ESSENTIAL TIPS

101

BASIC
GARDENING

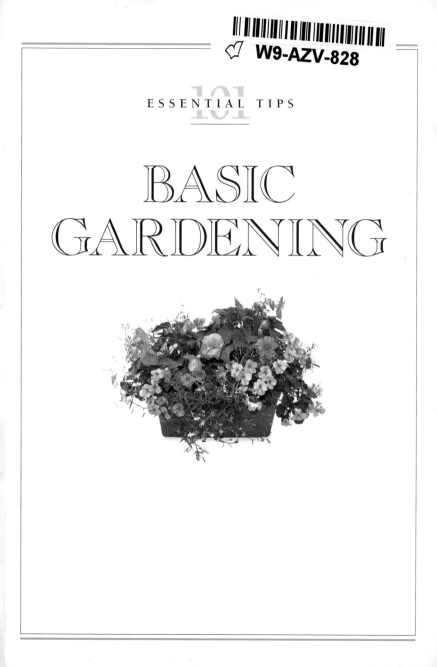

ESSENTIAL TIPS

BASIC GARDENING

Pippa Greenwood

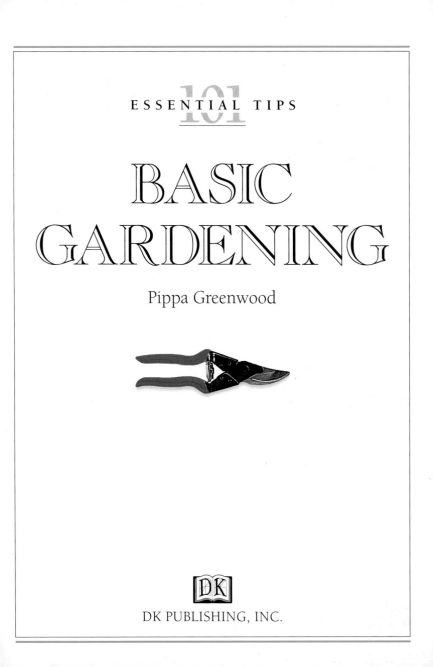

DK PUBLISHING, INC.

A DK PUBLISHING BOOK

Editor Polly Boyd
Art Editor Mason Linklater
Senior Editor Gillian Roberts
Series Art Editor Alison Donovan
Production Controller Jenny May
US Editor Ray Rogers

First American Edition 1998
4 6 8 10 9 7 5 3
Published in the United States by DK Publishing, Inc.
95 Madison Avenue, New York, New York 10016

Visit us on the World Wide Web at http://www.dk.com

ISBN 0-7894-2777-X

Text film output by R&B Creative Services Ltd, Great Britain
Reproduced by Colourscan, Singapore
Printed and bound in Italy by Graphicom

ESSENTIAL TIPS

KNOW YOUR GARDEN

1 MAKING THE MOST OF YOUR GARDEN

The key to a successful garden is careful planning. Before you embark on any practical gardening, familiarize yourself with the site – its soil type, climate, and exposure – and the needs of different plants. Consider what you have to work with, and be realistic in your aims.

LOOK AROUND
If you have just moved to a new area, take a look at neighboring gardens in order to get an idea of the growing conditions and kinds of plants that are likely to thrive in your own garden.

SUMMER SCENE
When planning your garden, select plants of varied heights. Wide borders encourage more diversity than narrow ones.

2 EXPOSURE

Before planting, consider the topography of your garden and the direction in which it faces. Is it very shady, or does it receive a considerable amount of sun most of the day? Is it sheltered by large trees or buildings? Observe where sun and shade fall in your garden throughout the day (and year, if possible), and select plants accordingly (*Tip 7*).

SUNNY BORDER
Opium poppies, foxgloves, gladioli, geraniums, and pinks flourish in this sunny border. However, many other plants prefer a shadier site.

3 CLIMATE

Weather conditions dictate the kinds of plants that will grow successfully in your garden. In a frost-prone climate, tender or marginally hardy plants, as well as young shoots and blossoms, are likely to be killed or damaged in autumn, winter, and spring. Excessive heat, humidity, wind, rain, and drought also damage many plants. Always read plant labels carefully, and choose plants that will thrive where you live.

COASTAL GARDEN
Salt-laden winds can damage plants and kill them. In coastal areas, grow succulents and low-growing plants, since they are fairly tolerant of drying winds.

4 MICROCLIMATES

Most gardens contain a range of different, perhaps extreme, growing conditions. There may be warm areas, such as a sunny border or wall, while other parts will be in dense shade. Shade is frequently described in terms of dry shade (the areas that are adjacent to tree trunks or walls) or moist shade – often found at the base of a shaded slope, or in areas that lack sun because of overhanging trees. Some parts of the garden may be particularly exposed to wind.

▷ **DRY SHADE**
A tree deprives the area directly beneath it of moisture and light, usually resulting in dry, shady growing conditions.

Foliage prevents most rain from reaching soil

Roots absorb moisture from soil

▷ **FROST POCKETS**
Low-lying areas, such as valleys, hollows, or the bases of slopes, are very frost prone. Frost pockets are also found behind dense hedges or walls.

Cold air sinks to lowest point

Frost builds up behind a dense hedge

Corner where two walls meet is particularly warm

Soil at wall base tends to be dry

AIR POLLUTION
Gardens alongside busy roads often suffer from pollution. Plant densely around the garden's edge to reduce the impact.

◁ **HEAT TRAPS**
Certain sunny, sheltered areas can often be very warm. Walls, in particular, retain heat and protect from cooling winds.

◁ *Acidic soil is indicated by the water turning yellow-orange.*

▷ *Neutral soil produces a bright green result.*

▷ *Alkaline soil turns the water bluish or dark green.*

5 WHAT IS YOUR SOIL pH?

When selecting plants, it is essential to know the pH of your soil – the extent of its acidity or alkalinity – since this will influence which plants you can and cannot grow (*Tip 7*). Soil pH is measured on a scale of 1–14.

- Acidic soil: pH value below 7.
- Neutral soil: pH value of 7.
- Alkaline soil: pH value above 7.

Do-it-yourself soil-testing kits are widely available: just collect a sample of soil from your garden, add water, and test. In many kits, the result is indicated by the water changing color (*see left*).

6 IDENTIFYING THE SOIL TEXTURE

The ideal garden soil is a medium loam – moisture-retentive yet well drained, and with a fine, crumbly texture. However, many soils have a very high clay or sand content. Clay soil is usually fertile but does not drain well, so roots may become waterlogged. Sandy soil is free-draining, lower in fertility, and easier to work.

TAKING ACTION
Some plants will not thrive in a sandy or clay soil, so choose plants carefully to suit your soil type (Tip 7). You can improve the texture of your soil by adding organic matter (Tip 19).

▷ CLAY SOIL
If the soil feels sticky and smooth, and you can mold it when it is wet, it is likely to have a high clay content.

▷ SANDY SOIL
Paler in color than a clay soil, sandy soil is also lighter and looser in texture and feels rough and gritty when rubbed.

CHOOSING PLANTS

7 KEY CONSIDERATIONS

A flourishing garden depends on putting the right plant in the right place. Mistakes can be costly, so consider your site and select plants accordingly (*see chart below*). Plants needing acidic soil will not thrive anywhere else; those listed under alkaline tolerate soil with a high pH. The other categories indicate which plants can tolerate certain soil textures, exposures, or microclimates (*Tip 4*).

CHOOSING THE RIGHT PLANT

Acidic soil	Alkaline soil	Sandy soil	Clay soil
Arctostaphylos	*Acanthus*	*Abutilon* (some)	*Aucuba*
Calluna	*Alchemilla*	*Achillea*	*Clematis*
Camellia	*Anemone*	*Artemisia*	*Cornus*
Daboecia	*Aquilegia*	*Ceanothus*	*Cotoneaster*
Erica	*Artemisia*	*Cistus*	*Forsythia*
Fothergilla	*Bergenia*	*Cotinus*	*Geranium* (hardy,
Gaultheria	*Campanula*	*Cytisus*	herbaceous sorts)
Hamamelis	*Ceanothus*	*Elaeagnus*	*Helleborus*
Kalmia	*Chaenomeles*	*Jasminum* (hardy	*Hosta*
Magnolia (some)	*Clematis*	sorts)	*Kerria*
Nomocharis	*Fuchsia*	*Kerria*	*Laburnum*
Nyssa	*Kerria*	*Laburnum*	*Lonicera* (some)
Phyllodoce	*Lonicera*	*Lavandula*	*Philadelphus*
Rhododendron	*Matthiola*	*Mahonia*	*Prunus*
Vaccinium	*Pyracantha*	*Perovskia*	*Rosa*
	Syringa	*Rosmarinus*	*Sedum*
	Tulipa	*Sorbus*	*Syringa*
	Viburnum	*Verbascum*	*Viburnum*
	Weigela	*Wisteria*	*Wisteria*

ASTER NOVAE-ANGLIAE

POISONOUS PLANTS
*The label should identify
a plant that is harmful if
eaten or touched. Avoid
toxic plants if you have
children or pets.*

FERNS, HOSTAS, & BERGENIAS IN MOIST, DAPPLED SHADE

Dry shade	Moist shade	Sunny sites	Exposed sites
Alchemilla mollis	*Anemone blanda*	*Achillea*	*Achillea*
Anemone nemorosa	*Aucuba*	*Arabis*	*Anaphalis*
Aucuba	*Bergenia*	*Aster*	*Artemisia*
Buxus sempervirens	*Camellia japonica*	*Aubrieta*	*Berberis*
Cyclamen	*& cultivars*	*Campsis radicans*	*Choisya ternata*
Daphne laureola	*Convallaria majalis*	*Cistus*	*Crocus*
Epimedium	*Digitalis*	*Cytisus*	*Cytisus*
Euonymus	*Eranthis*	*Eryngium*	*Dianthus*
Ilex, many species &	*Erythronium*	*Fremontodendron*	*Erigeron*
cultivars	*Fritillaria* (most)	*Genista*	*Euonymus fortunei*
Iris foetidissima	*Galanthus nivalis*	*Hypericum*	*& cultivars*
Lonicera japonica	*Helleborus*	*Iberis*	*Geranium* (hardy,
'Halliana'	*Hosta*	*Phlomis*	herbaceous types)
Mahonia	*Lonicera*	*Rosmarinus*	*Ilex opaca &*
Pulmonaria	*Matteuccia*	*Santolina*	cultivars
Ranunculus ficaria	*Pieris*	*Sedum*	*Narcissus*
& cultivars	*Primula* (most)	*Senecio*	*Pyracantha*
Tellima grandiflora	*Rhododendron*	*Tamarix*	*Rosa rugosa*
Vinca	*Skimmia japonica*	*Yucca*	*Viburnum tinus*

8 WHEN TO BUY PLANTS

Once you have considered carefully the plants that are likely to thrive in your garden, and your overall planting plan, you are ready to buy. However, remember that certain times of year are better buying times than others.

- Never buy plants during or just after a very cold spell. The root balls, even of very hardy plants, may freeze if they are unprotected. This can kill the plant.
- Avoid buying plants before the spring if possible: new foliage gives an indication of the plant's health.
- Spring is the best time to buy perennials, since there is generally more choice at this time.

9 HOW PLANTS ARE SOLD

Many plants are sold in containers: they may be container-grown or containerized (see below). Bare-root plants, usually roses, are raised in the open ground and are lifted and sold when dormant, with no soil around their roots. Balled-and-burlapped plants are sold with roots and soil wrapped in burlap.

Strong, fibrous, well-developed roots

◁ CONTAINERIZED SHRUB
Unlike container-grown plants, these are raised in open ground and are lifted and potted up for sale.

△ CONTAINER-GROWN SHRUB
Container-grown plants are raised and sold in pots. They usually establish more easily than other kinds, since their root systems are more developed.

Soil mix falls away when pot is removed

PLANTS BY MAIL
Many nurseries sell plants by mail, and may be highly specialized in their offerings. Open packages immediately upon receipt.

10 SELECTING ANNUALS

Annuals are non-woody plants that germinate, flower, set seed, and die within one year. Since they last only a short period of time, it is particularly important to choose healthy specimens. There should be no sign of *Botrytis* (*Tip 64*), and the roots should be well developed but not pot-bound or discolored. The most economical way to buy annuals is as young seedlings in trays, or as plugs in flats. They are often available in small pots.

△ **WEAK PLANTS**
The stems are straggly and the leaves are sparse; many have fungal growth.

△ LATHYRUS
ODORATUS
'JANE AMANDA'

Sturdy stems and unyellowed leaves

New buds developing

Compact, vigorous growth

Soil mix is moist, with no sign of algae or weeds

▽ SEEDLING PLUG

Strong, uncongested roots

△ **HEALTHY ANNUALS**
These pansies are fine examples of thriving annuals. There is no sign of rot on the leaves or roots.

15

11 SELECTING PERENNIALS

Perennials are mainly herbaceous plants that die down at the end of the year, lie dormant over winter, and produce new growth the following spring. Most are sold in containers. It is best to buy them in spring, since you can inspect them in full growth. If purchasing when dormant, check that the crown is firm and undamaged. If buying in early spring, ensure that there are plenty of strong buds or shoots.

△ **WEAK GROWTH**
The top-growth is sparse and the soil mix is falling away, indicating undeveloped roots.

△ **POT-BOUND**
The roots are highly congested and the foliage is unhealthy and discolored.

▷ **HEALTHY LUPINE**
This lupine is a fine example of a thriving perennial. New growth is apparent, the foliage is healthy, and there is no sign of pests or diseases.

Healthy green top-growth

Sturdy new shoots

Moist, weed-free soil mix

CHECK THE ROOTS
When buying perennials, always turn them out to examine their roots. White roots indicate a healthy plant with new growth; blackened ones indicate that the plant has experienced moisture or nutrient stress.

Strong roots visible, but not congested

Undamaged nose; no new growth

12 SELECTING BULBS

Bulbs are underground storage organs, formed from modified leaves or leaf bases. Each year they produce new leaves that die down after flowering. Rhizomes, tubers, and corms are botanically quite distinct but are all treated as bulbs. Look for the same qualities when buying, either loose or in packages.

Intact tunic

Firm base; no new growth

△ **HEALTHY DAFFODIL**
Select bulbs that have not yet started into growth and are free from blemishes and signs of pest attack. They should feel firm.

▷ **POOR SPECIMEN**
Twin-nosed bulbs produce two plants. However, if the second bulb is small, it may not flower well.

Offset too small to flower in first year

13 SELECTING A ROSE

Roses are perennial, woody plants. They are usually sold bare-root or containerized when dormant, and container-grown in the growing season (*Tip 9*). Buy a bare-root rose only if you can plant or heel it in immediately (*Tip 21*).

Healthy, firm, plump buds

◁ **UNHEALTHY ROSE**
The roots of this bare-root rose will not anchor the plant and will fail to absorb moisture and nutrients.

▷ **HEALTHY ROSE**
This bare-root rose has evenly spaced, sturdy branches (none are crossed) and a well-developed root system.

Roots severely cut back

Even, strong, unbroken roots

14 SELECTING A SHRUB

Shrubs are perennial, deciduous or evergreen, woody plants; they tend to be bushy and multi-stemmed. They are usually container-grown but are also available containerized, bare-root, or balled-and-burlapped (*Tip 9*). When buying a shrub, always examine the roots, especially if the plant is not in leaf, since it will tell you a lot about its condition: healthy roots are white and firm. Look also at the soil mix: it should be free of algae, weeds, and liverworts.

△ UNHEALTHY SPECIMEN
Twiggy and sparse, with extremely congested roots, this Prostanthera cuneata *has made little growth and would be a poor purchase.*

Well-spaced top-growth

◁ HEALTHY SKIMMIA
Unlike the example shown above, the stems, foliage, and roots of this skimmia are evenly distributed, vigorous, and healthy.

Green, healthy foliage

Numerous firm, fibrous roots

SMALL IS BEST
Young shrubs are not only more economical, they are usually easier to establish and grow more quickly than larger plants.

15 SELECTING A TREE

Trees are perennial, deciduous or evergreen, woody plants, usually with a single stem. They are generally the largest and longest-lived plants. You can buy trees in various forms: container-grown, containerized, bare-root, and balled-and-burlapped (*Tip 9*). When choosing a tree, beware of severely pruned specimens: most trees do not need much pruning, and it may mean that the plant is unhealthy or has suffered dieback.

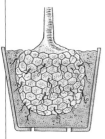

△ ROOTS IN MESH
If you purchase a tree in a container with its roots in mesh, cut the mesh and soak the root ball before planting.

▷ BALLED-&-
BURLAPPED TREE
When buying a balled-and-burlapped tree, select a plant with a large root ball. Squeeze it to ensure that the soil is moist and firm.

Intact burlap prevents soil from drying out

16 BUYING SEEDS

When you purchase seeds, always check the sell-by date to ensure that they are completely fresh. Most seeds are viable for about one year only, although seeds in sealed packets may last several years. Check the conditions in which they have been stored: a cool, dry environment is the ideal. If exposed to direct sunlight, they may deteriorate. Many seeds are F1 hybrids. These produce larger flowers or crops but are more expensive. Some seed is partially pre-germinated, which makes germination rates more rapid.

BEFORE PLANTING

17 BASIC TOOLS & EQUIPMENT

The sheer range of tools available can be a daunting sight to the novice gardener. However, you need only a few basic tools to start with (*shown here*), and you can expand your collection in time. Before buying tools, test them for size, weight, and comfort.

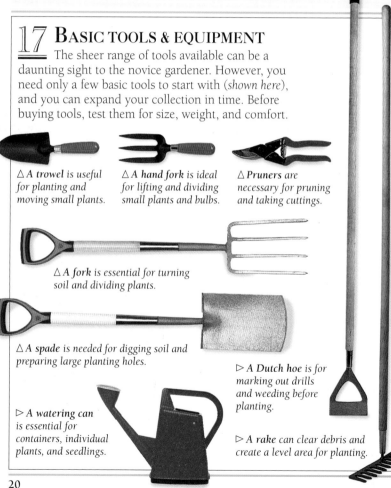

△ *A* **trowel** *is useful for planting and moving small plants.*

△ *A* **hand fork** *is ideal for lifting and dividing small plants and bulbs.*

△ **Pruners** *are necessary for pruning and taking cuttings.*

△ *A* **fork** *is essential for turning soil and dividing plants.*

△ *A* **spade** *is needed for digging soil and preparing large planting holes.*

▷ *A* **Dutch hoe** *is for marking out drills and weeding before planting.*

▷ *A* **watering can** *is essential for containers, individual plants, and seedlings.*

▷ *A* **rake** *can clear debris and create a level area for planting.*

18 HOW TO LOOK AFTER YOUR TOOLS

Tools will last for many years if you look after them correctly. Store them in a dry place, and never leave them out in the rain. Clean off soil and debris after use, and oil metal tools to prevent rust. Stainless-steel tools will not rust, but they are more expensive than coated-steel ones.

19 IMPROVING YOUR SOIL

You'll improve the texture of your soil to some degree just by digging and forking. However, to make substantial improvements to soil texture, moisture retention, drainage, or fertility, incorporating organic and inorganic matter before you plant is a must.

△ GRAVEL

▷ COARSE SAND

△ PEAT

△ LIME

◁ SOIL pH
Peat or peat substitutes increase acidity and benefit sandy soils. Lime is alkaline and is good for clay soils.

△ SOIL TEXTURE
Add coarse horticultural sand and gravel to lighten heavy clay soils and improve drainage. Never use builder's materials.

▷ SOIL IMPROVERS
Organic materials improve moisture retention, texture, and drainage. Dig them in, or use them as a mulch.

△ LEAFMOLD

△ COIR

△ MANURE

IMPROVING HEAVY SOILS
Dig heavy clay soils in autumn. If the soil is dug and left clear over winter, frost will break down large lumps. Avoid digging in wet weather, since it will cause the soil to compact.

△ COMPOSTED BARK

△ ORGANIC MATTER

20 MAKING COMPOST

Compost made at home from organic kitchen and garden waste will greatly improve the quality of your soil, and is highly economical. It will take at least three to four months to make. Ensure it is fully rotted before use, and follow these guidelines:

- Add the waste in thin layers: up to 6in (15cm) is best.
- Include a mixture of materials: moist and dry; bulky and light; kitchen and garden waste.
- Turn it once a week.
- Keep it well insulated in winter, and add water in summer.

PRECAUTIONS
Do not use meat and other pungent foods for compost, since they will attract vermin. Also avoid putting in perennial weeds and diseased plants. Use grass in moderation.

COMPOST BIN
Whatever sort of compost bin you choose, it must provide easy access for turning and removing compost. This model has a removable panel.

21 STORING PLANTS BEFORE PLANTING

Always aim to transfer newly acquired plants to the soil as soon as possible. However, this is not always practical: perhaps it's too cold or wet to plant, or time runs out. Plants may be stored for a few days, but their roots are highly vulnerable, particularly in extreme weather conditions. Bulbs have special needs (*Tip 31*).

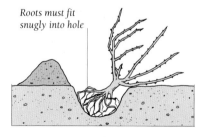

Roots must fit snugly into hole

HEELING IN
To protect a bare-root tree or shrub temporarily, place it at an angle in a hole in the ground. Backfill the hole.

PLUNGE METHOD
Protect container-grown plants by plunging them into the soil while still in their pots. Keep them moist, but do not overwater.

PLANTING

22 WHEN TO PLANT

Ideal planting times are:
- Container-grown shrubs and trees: spring and autumn.
- Balled-and-burlapped trees: spring, autumn, and late winter.
- Bare-root roses: end of autumn or, in cold-winter areas, early spring.
- Perennials: any time, except in extreme weather conditions.
- Annuals: late spring and early summer.
- Bulbs: soon after obtaining.

PLANT WHEN THE TIME IS RIGHT

23 PLANTING SHRUBS & OTHER PLANTS

Get your plant off to a good start by using the correct planting technique. Ensure that you plant at the correct depth: a common mistake is to plant too deep. If the plant is pot-bound, gently tease out girdling roots, and cut back any that are damaged or restricted.

1 Dig a hole about twice the size of the root ball of the plant. Water the hole well, then let the water drain away.

2 Soak the plants, then position each in its hole at the correct depth (*Tip 27*). Backfill with soil, compost, and fertilizer.

3 Gently firm the soil, and water well. Lay 2–3in (5–7cm) of mulch around the root area; leave the stem area clear.

24 WHY MULCH?

A mulch benefits the garden in several ways. It helps prevent the soil from drying out and also keeps weeds in check by depriving them of light. Apply a 2–3in (5–7cm) layer of mulch around plants at planting, and again in autumn or spring. Manure or bark chips are common, but many household items may also be used.

◁ USING CARPET
Save any carpet scraps, and place them around plants. Cover with a thin layer of bark chips.

▷ USING NEWSPAPER
Soak newspaper in water. Lay the wet paper around the plant, and cover it up with a layer of soil.

25 PLANTING ANNUALS

Correct planting is a must for annuals. They need to establish quickly, since their lifespan is no more than a year, and they need to look their best in the short time that they're in flower. Annuals are easy to grow from seed, but you can also purchase plants closer to flowering time. Water, feed, and deadhead annuals regularly.

BEFORE YOU PLANT
Water the plant tray well and push up the bases to release the seedling plugs. Plant immediately.

AFTER YOU PLANT
Water thoroughly after planting, then spray the leaves with a foliar feed. This will encourage growth.

PLANTING OUT
Plant annuals on cool, overcast, non-windy days. The best time to plant is early evening, to allow time for the roots to establish. Avoid planting in the heat of midday.

26 PLANTING PERENNIALS

Groups of one kind of perennial tend to look better than individual plants dotted at random along a border. When planting in groups, consider the potential heights and spreads of perennials before you begin, and leave a comfortable distance between plants.

PLANNING A BORDER
When newly planted, a herbaceous border can look sparse. Fill in gaps with bulbs and annuals.

PRUNE TO PROTECT
In hot weather, reduce moisture loss by pruning off flowers and the oldest leaves before planting.

27 PLANTING DEPTH

Most perennials should be planted so that the top of the root ball is at the soil surface. However, some perform better if they are planted slightly higher or deeper, depending on whether they need well-drained or moist conditions. Tuberous-rooted plants dry out easily, and so require deep planting.

SOIL LEVEL
This is the usual planting depth: the crown of the plant is set level with the surrounding soil.

RAISED PLANTING
For plants that rot at the crown, and variegated plants that tend to revert, set them slightly above the ground.

SHALLOW PLANTING
Plant perennials that require plenty of moisture so that the crowns are 1in (2.5cm) below ground level.

DEEP PLANTING
Perennials with tuberous roots require deep planting: plant the crowns 4in (10cm) below ground level.

AVOID DROUGHT
For hot, dry areas that are especially vulnerable to drought, it is best to use the shallow planting method.

28 PLANTING BULBS

Most bulbs thrive in a well-drained, sunny site. They generally look best in informal groups, rather than in straight, regimented rows. Allow the leaves to die down of their own accord to ensure healthy plants next year. To avoid having yellowing foliage on display, plant the bulbs in a basket, which you can lift after flowering.

▽ PLANTING IN GROUPS
Several bulbs may be planted in one hole. This saves time and creates a more natural, informal display, especially if groups of odd numbers are used.

◁ PLANTING SINGLY
Plant each bulb in a separate hole at the correct depth (Tip 29). Cover with soil and gently firm it down.

1 Dig a large hole in well-prepared ground. Put the bulbs, tips upward, at the correct distances apart (*Tip 29*).

2 When all the bulbs are in position, gently draw the soil over them with your hand until the ground is level.

3 With the back of a rake, press down the soil over the planting area. Do not tread on the soil: this could harm the tips.

29 PLANTING DEPTH FOR BULBS

The size of bulb determines the planting depth: most bulbs need to be planted at a depth between three and five times their height. If winters are very cold or summers particularly dry, they must be planted even deeper.

Planting distances are usually two to three bulb widths apart. Always check the instructions on the package for depths and distances. If you are planting bulbs in a basket (*Tip 28*), place the top of the basket just below soil level.

30 PLANTING IN WET OR DRY SOIL

Bulbs will not thrive if your soil is very wet or heavy. Equally, if the soil is extremely dry, the bulbs will not flower properly and may even die. A small layer of grit or compost placed at the base of the planting hole or trench improves the texture of the soil, and provides better drainage or moisture retention as required.

◁ WET SOIL
A 1in (2.5cm) layer of coarse grit improves drainage.

▷ DRY SOIL
A 1½in (3.5cm) layer of moist compost improves moisture retention.

31 STORING BULBS

Always try to plant bulbs right away if possible. However, the conditions may not be suitable for planting, or you may wish to move bulbs already in a border elsewhere the following season. Store them in a cool, dry place: a frost-free shed, garage, or greenhouse is ideal.

LABELING
To avoid any muddle or confusion, always keep different kinds of bulbs in separate bags, and label them clearly.

1 When the foliage turns yellow after flowering, lift the bulbs with a fork and place in labeled containers.

2 Clean the soil off the bulbs and rub off any flaking tissue. Discard dying leaves and diseased or damaged bulbs.

3 Place the bulbs on a wire tray so that they do not touch. Leave overnight, dust with fungicide, and store in paper bags.

32 PLANTING A BARE-ROOT ROSE

The end of autumn is the best time to plant roses; alternatively, in areas with cold winters, plant in early spring. If possible, plant them immediately after receipt; if not, heel them in (*Tip 21*). Before planting, check the roots: if they seem dry, soak them in water for an hour or two. Remove any roots that are withered, damaged, diseased, or dead, and prune by about one-third any that are very long or thick.

1 △ Before you plant, prune out diseased, damaged, or dead stems, and any that are straggly or crossing. The stems should be evenly spaced.

2 ▷ Hold the rose in the hole; spread the roots. Lay a stake across the hole. The graft union should be 1in (2.5cm) below the stake. Backfill, firm, water.

33 PLANTING & STAKING A TREE

You may need to stake trees and large shrubs at planting to prevent windrock (*Tip 68*). Prepare for planting (*Tip 23*). To stake trees, drive the stake into the hole before inserting the tree. In windy areas, stake the tree on the windward side. For balled-and-burlapped trees, place in the hole, water the root ball, loosen and push down the burlap or mesh, and backfill the hole. Then put in the stake.

1 ◁ Drive a stake into the hole just off center. Slide the tree out of its pot and spread out the roots.

2 ▷ Place the tree in the hole, close to the stake. Spread the roots. Check the level with a stake. Backfill, firm, water.

34 PLANTING CLIMBERS

A common mistake when planting climbers is to place them too close to a wall or fence, where the roots are in the "rainshadow" – the area of ground that is sheltered from rain by the wall or fence. Most climbers will not thrive in very dry soil. Make sure your planting hole is 12–18in (30–45cm) from the support. The support's base should be 12in (30cm) above the soil and 2in (5cm) from the wall or fence.

△ CLEMATIS 'BEES' JUBILEE'

1 △ Prepare a large planting hole. Loosen the soil at the base and add a little compost.

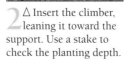

2 △ Insert the climber, leaning it toward the support. Use a stake to check the planting depth.

3 △ Spread the roots and backfill the hole with soil, organic matter, and fertilizer. Firm well.

4 △ Select 4 or 5 strong shoots. Insert a stake for each, tie them to the support, tie in the shoots.

5 △ Using a sharp pair of pruners, remove weak, damaged, or dead stems to the central stem.

6 △ Water the plant and soil well. Apply a 2–3in (5–8cm) layer of mulch, avoiding the stems.

35 SUPPORTING CLIMBERS

Some climbers – Virginia creeper or ivy, for example – are self-clinging and need no support. However, most need netting, wires, or a trellis to keep them in place.

The extent of support depends on the size and weight of the climber. Always use good-quality rust-proof hardware, and ensure that you put in enough, or the support may fail.

▽ TRELLIS
For light- or medium-weight climbers, a trellis is ideal. Attach it to hinged wooden battens to provide access to the wall.

△ NETTING
A system of wire or plastic netting, combined with U-shaped staples, supports permanent lightweight and annual climbers.

△ GALVANIZED WIRE
Vigorous or heavy climbers require the support of heavy-duty wires. Vine eyes hold the wires in place.

36 PLANTING IN PAVING & CREVICES

Plants liven up a patio with their colors and shapes, and also reduce infiltration from weeds. Remove any broken slabs and plant small shrubs in the soil beneath. Alternatively, sow seeds in crevices between paving, or in gaps between stones or bricks in walls.

◁ PATIO PLANTING
Remove any crushed gravel and plant in a mixture of soil and compost.

▷ SOFTENED LANDSCAPE
The subtle colors and moundlike forms of these plants break up the hard edges of the paving stones.

37 MOVING ESTABLISHED PLANTS

If a plant is not thriving in its present position, seriously consider moving it – it could well fare better elsewhere. Young, small shrubs are always easier to move than older, more established ones. Perennials, bulbs, and rhizomes may be divided and moved (*Tips 77–79*); transplant in spring or autumn, before the onset of very dry or cold weather. Established shrubs are best moved in autumn.

TRANSPLANTING A SHRUB
Young shrubs can usually be moved fairly easily when dormant, but established shrubs need to be lifted out with a large ball of soil around their roots. Prepare the new hole before lifting the shrub.

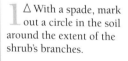
1 △ With a spade, mark out a circle in the soil around the extent of the shrub's branches.

2 △ Dig a trench around the circle, then gently loosen the soil around the root ball with a fork.

3 △ Undercut the root ball with a spade, cutting through woody roots if necessary.

4 △ Lift the root ball onto a piece of burlap, pull the burlap around it, and tie securely.

5 △ Transport the shrub wrapped in burlap to its newly prepared planting hole.

6 △ Carefully remove the burlap and replant the shrub in the usual way (*Tip 23*).

WATERING & FEEDING

38 HOW TO WATER

For plants to grow (and to avoid waste), it's essential to water them correctly. Water the surface of very dry soil only lightly to prevent water from running off the surface; water again when it has been absorbed. Avoid watering in the heat of midday. It can cause damage, and the resulting humidity may lead to diseases.

◁ USING A POT
To water a large plant, sink a pot with a drainage hole into the soil near a plant and fill with water.

▷ USING A HOSE
Water the depression around a plant. Never aim a jet at the plant's base.

39 FIVE WATER-SAVING TIPS

1 Use water-retaining gel granules: they conserve moisture and release it back into the soil.
2 Collect and use rainwater: install a water barrel or similar container at the base of a downspout. Both must be kept clean.
3 Recycle water from a bathtub or sink. Do not use water from a washing machine or dishwasher – the detergents may be harmful.

4 Improve moisture retention by adding organic matter to the soil (*Tip 19*) and a layer of mulch (*Tip 24*), particularly on sandy soils.
5 During hot weather, move containers to a partly shaded area, out of full sun. Use planters that are designed to supply water on demand.

40 VULNERABLE PLANTS

Some plants require frequent watering:
- Plants with shallow roots, such as annuals.
- Newly planted plants.
- Seedlings and young plants.
- Leafy vegetables; fruiting crops; peas, beans, and other legumes; tree, bush, and cane fruit.
- Shrubs such as *Camellia* and *Rhododendron*, whose buds form at the end of the summer for the following spring.

CAMELLIA
Water camellias well in the summer, or they will not flower well next year.

41 WHY FEED YOUR PLANTS?

Most plants need additional feeding to grow well. The chart below shows which plants and soil types benefit from adding specific nutrients. Other minor nutrients may also be beneficial.

PLANTS, SOILS, & NUTRIENTS

Nutrient	Plants in need	Soils in need	Signs of shortage
Nitrogen	All plants, especially those grown for foliage.	Most soils after heavy cropping, but mainly poor soils.	Pale leaves and unhealthy-looking growth.
Phosphorus	All plants, especially newly planted plants and bulbs.	Most soils after heavy cropping, but mostly sandy or poor soils.	Poor root development, indicated by stunted growth.
Potassium	All plants, especially those grown for flowers or fruit.	All soils, especially those with plenty of added high-nitrogen fertilizer or manure.	Poor flowering and fruiting; plants are very prone to cold damage.
Magnesium	All plants, since this is a main constituent of chlorophyll.	Sandy, acidic, or wet soils, and after excessive use of potassium fertilizers.	Yellow or brown patches at the leaf edges and between leaf veins.
Iron	All plants, especially acid-loving plants, e.g. *Rhododendron*.	All soils, especially those with a high pH caused by limestone and lime.	Yellowing between the leaf veins, especially on younger growth.

42 FERTILIZER FORMS

There are various forms of fertilizer available. Choose one that suits the specific needs of your plants and the time of year. Consider also the size of your garden and the amount of time you have to spare. Ensure that you water fertilizers in well after applying, or the plants will not absorb their nutrients.

▷ SLOW-
RELEASE PELLETS

GRANULES
Scatter fertilizer granules over the whole soil surface or around the bases of plants (Tip 45).

◁ GRANULAR FERTILIZER

43 BASIC FERTILIZERS

Most soils require regular additions of nitrogen for healthy foliage, phosphorus (phosphate) for strong roots, and potassium (potash) for flowering and fruiting. Other fertilizers provide valuable nutrients for specific deficiencies, soil types, or plants. Organic fertilizers are usually bulkier and less concentrated than inorganic ones, but they often improve soil texture.

△ *Bonemeal is a good, slow-release source of phosphorus. It has a high level of alkalinit*

◁ *Potassium sulfate has a high potassium content. Apply it to flowerbeds in autumn and early spring.*

▷ *Ammonium sulfate contains concentrated nitrogen. Later in the season, use in moderation.*

△ *Wood ash may be collected from a fireplace after burning plant material. It contains potassium.*

▽ **LIQUID & SOLUBLE FERTILIZERS**
*For rapid effect, use one of these
fertilizers. Most are applied
to the roots, but some
may be applied to
the leaves.*

△ **FERTILIZER STICKS**   △ **FERTILIZER TABLETS**

△ **STICKS & TABLETS**
*Insert fertilizer sticks and tablets
into the soil or soil mix around the
bases of plants.*

△ **SOLUBLE FERTILIZER**

◁ **LIQUID FERTILIZER**

△ **Fish, blood, & bonemeal** *is
a concentrated general
fertilizer. It contains nitrogen,
phosphorus, and potassium.*

△ **Mushroom compost**
*contains a range of
nutrients and also
improves soil texture.*

△ **Manure** *is a beneficial
source of nitrogen and
trace elements.*

▽ **Liquid seaweed extract** *contains
nitrogen, phosphorus, and potassium.
Apply it to the soil or leaves.*

44 WHEN TO FEED

Feeding should take place
during a period of active growth.
Beware of feeding too late in the
season. It could promote soft
growth, which may be damaged
by early frosts. The exact timing
depends on the kind of fertilizer
you use and the needs of the
plant. Avoid feeding in hot, dry
weather or heavy rain.

45 HOW TO APPLY FERTILIZER

Fertilizers are applied in different ways, depending on the form you choose (*Tip 42*). Always read the manufacturer's instructions: the type, quantities, and timing are crucial to a plant's success. Keep a separate watering can specifically for applying fertilizers, and do so with care: use gloves and avoid breathing in vapor or dust.

FORKING IN
Scatter fertilizer granules around the base of the plant and fork them into the soil, taking care not to damage the roots. Water them in well.

46 FEEDING SEEDLINGS

You may find that your seedlings start looking unhealthy, owing to lack of nutrients in the soil mix. If you are unable to prick them out immediately, apply a suitable foliar feed to the leaves and roots. Treat seedlings with care, since they can be very delicate.

FEEDING TECHNIQUE
Apply using a small watering can or mister. Do not drench the seedlings.

47 CARING FOR BULBS

Bulbs are generally easy to look after. They require only a little care to ensure they flower well year after year. You will need to water them, and they will benefit from feeding, particularly naturalized bulbs and those that have been in the same place for a long time. A liquid feed, applied to the leaves (see right) after flowering, will provide the bulbs with sufficient nutrients so that they flower well the following year.

YELLOWING LEAVES
Allow bulbs to die back naturally. Do not tie or cut the foliage for at least six weeks: it will deprive the bulb of nutrients.

FOLIAR FEED
Use a watering can with a rose cap to apply a liquid feed every 10–14 days after flowering. Continue until the leaves begin to turn yellow and die back (about six weeks).

WEEDING

48 WHY & WHEN TO WEED

It is vital to remove weeds regularly, starting in early spring. They deprive other plants of nutrients, water, and light, and can be invasive, colonizing the garden. Deal with them promptly, before they have a chance to set seed.

THRIVING BORDER
The plants in this well-maintained border are flourishing. They do not need to compete with weeds for sustenance or light.

49 PREVENTING WEEDS

There is much you can do to discourage weeds from growing in your garden. One of the most effective ways is to deprive them of light – an essential element for growth. Close planting and a mulch around the bases of plants keep weeds at bay, but remove all annual and perennial weeds from the soil before applying a mulch.

GRAVEL MULCH
A 2in (5cm) layer of coarse gravel around plants keeps weeds away.

USING GROUNDCOVER
Plant dense-growing groundcover around plants to suppress weed growth.

COMPOSTING WEEDS
Do not add weeds that have set seed or those that are particularly pernicious to a compost pile or bin. Some can regenerate and return to your garden, even if they have been chopped up.

50 WEEDING EQUIPMENT

In order to maintain your garden and effectively eliminate weeds, you will need to invest in a few basic tools. Weeds are controlled in a variety of different ways: a combination of cultivation and chemical methods is often necessary. The tools shown here are useful for clearing weeds in most areas. The tool you use depends on the kind of weed and where it is growing.

◁ *A Dutch hoe clears surface weeds without damaging other plants.*

◁ *An onion hoe helps to weed between closely spaced plants.*

◁ *A patio weeder can get weeds out of crevices in paving.*

▽ *A dribble bar is attached to a watering can for applying weedkiller.*

▷ *A draw hoe is useful for chopping weeds in half.*

▷ *An asparagus knife is for weeding lawns.*

USING A DUTCH HOE
Skim a Dutch hoe across the surface of the soil around plants to remove annual weeds.

51 WEEDING BY HAND

Weeding should be carried out at the right time, and frequently, using the tools shown above. Here are some guidelines for successful weeding by hand.

- Always remove flowering weeds before they have time to set seed, and preferably before they begin to flower.
- Lift as much of the root system out of the ground as you can. Many weeds can regenerate from parts of root or stem left in the ground.
- If you are clearing a large area of weeds, begin by cutting off the flowerheads and seedheads to prevent seeds from entering the soil.

52 CHEMICAL WEEDKILLERS

For areas where it would be difficult or too labor intensive to weed by hand, use chemical weed-killers as a practical alternative.

They are available as sprays, soluble powders, gels, and liquids. Apply weedkiller as stated on the label, and follow safety precautions.

PAINT-ON GEL
For borders where hand-weeding or spraying would be difficult or damaging, use paint-on gel instead.

LIQUID WEEDKILLER
Apply liquid weedkiller, using a watering can and dribble bar attachment, on paths, patios, and drives.

WHEN TO APPLY
The best time to apply chemical weedkiller is when the weeds are growing actively. Do not use it in windy weather, since it may harm other plants. Avoid using it just before it rains, since rain may render it ineffective.

53 WEEDING UNCULTIVATED AREAS

You will probably need to use a combination of hand and chemical methods to clear a large, uncultivated area of weeds. If weed infestation is particularly heavy, use

a total weedkiller containing glyphosate. You may find that you require more than one application. Wait until there is good covering of growth before reapplying.

◁ **CLEARING WEEDS**
Fork out large, woody weeds. Remove the top-growth, and dig out as many roots as you can.

▷ **WEED PREVENTION**
Cover a weeded area with black plastic to prevent regrowth. Dig a trench to hold the plastic in place.

39

54 COMMON WEEDS

Annual weeds grow, flower, set seed, and die within one year. They grow rapidly, so remove them before they seed. Perennial weeds survive year after year. Many have fleshy roots that enable them to persist even if the top-growth is killed off. You can kill most weeds by digging out the whole root system or by using a weedkiller.

ANNUAL WEEDS

▷ **Hairy bittercress** develops quickly. Hoe before it sets seed, hand-weed, or cover with mulch.

◁ **Groundsel** is very fast growing. Hoe or hand-weed before it sets seed. Cover affected ground with mulch.

▷ **Common chickweed** can smother tiny plants. Hoe or hand-weed before it sets seed, then mulch.

◁ **Annual nettles** should be removed before the seeds develop. Hand-weed or spot-treat with a weedkiller such as glyphosate.

PERENNIAL WEEDS

▷ **Horsetail** is difficult to dig out, since its roots penetrate deep. Spot-treat with glyphosate.

◁ **Bindweed** can regenerate from sections of underground stem or root. Dig out repeatedly or apply glyphosate.

▷ **Quack grass** is invasive and spreads by creeping roots. Fork out, smother in black plastic, or use glyphosate.

◁ **Some oxalis species** have bulbils around the base, which divide to form new plants. Dig out in spring or treat with a weedkiller.

PRUNING

55 WHY PRUNE?

Pruning benefits plants in many ways. Most obviously, it keeps a plant at a manageable size and can enhance its shape. It may also improve the plant's performance – it encourages growth, flowering, or fruiting, and reduces the possibility of pests and diseases. For major pruning of trees, or removal of large branches, seek the expert help of an arborist.

OSMANTHUS DELAVAYI

56 BASIC EQUIPMENT

There is a variety of different tools for pruning. The tool you use depends on the nature and size of the plant you are pruning. Good-quality, sharp tools are essential: blunt tools can damage stems.

△ *A fold-up garden knife is convenient for light pruning tasks.*

◁ *Long-handled pruners are useful for inaccessible stems.*

▽ *A pruning saw is designed for branches over 1in (2.5cm) thick. Choose one with heat-treated, hardpoint teeth.*

▽ *Gardening gloves need to be sturdy to protect your hands.*

▽ *Pruners can cut soft and woody stems up to about ½in (1cm) thick.*

◁ *Shears are for trimming hedges and some woody plants.*

57 PRUNING SHRUBS

When to prune depends on when the shrub flowers and the age of the flower-producing stems. As a general rule, if a shrub flowers after midsummer, it should be pruned in winter or early spring. If it flowers earlier in the year, prune it immediately after flowering.

1 Using pruners, cut out any diseased, damaged, or dead wood back to healthy growth.

2 Remove up to one-third of the older wood. Cut it back to within 2–3in (5–8cm) of ground level.

3 Prune out any spindly, crossing, or weak growth to just above ground level.

PRUNING SEASONS

Winter or Early Spring		After Flowering	
Abutilon (some)	Hibiscus syriacus	Buddleja alternifolia	Magnolia (some)
Buddleja davidii	Hydrangea	Chaenomeles	Philadelphus
Caryopteris	Lavatera	Cotoneaster	Rhododendron
Ceanothus	Potentilla	Deutzia	Ribes sanguineum
Ceratostigma	Prunus triloba	Exochorda	Spiraea (some)
Cotinus	Spiraea (some)	Forsythia	Syringa
Fuchsia	Tamarix	Kerria	Weigela

58 CUTTING ANGLE

When pruning, it is extremely important to make the cut at the correct angle for the plant. If it has alternate shoots, cut at an angle; for opposite shoots, make a straight cut. Never cut too close or too far away from a bud: both can be detrimental.

Angled cut is for stems with alternate shoots or buds. Cut above the outward-facing shoot.

Straight cut is for pruning stems with opposite shoots or buds. Cut just above the shoots.

59 PRUNING ROSES

Most roses need regular pruning, usually between autumn and spring, to flower well and remain healthy. Instructions for general pruning are shown here, but roses also have specific needs, depending on their kind – a floribunda, hybrid tea, or climber, for example. Consult a specialist reference book or plant nursery for more detailed information.

ROSA 'LITTLE WHITE PET'

◁ **TIMELY PRUNING**
Cut out poor growth, shorten over-long stems, and cut back crossing branches regularly.

NEGLECTED ROSES
Excessive pruning of roses after years of neglect can prove fatal. If your roses have not been pruned regularly, prune them over two or three years.

Where to cut

Poor growth

Crossing branches

△ **POOR GROWTH**
Prune out any diseased, damaged, dead, or weak, spindly growth. It may spread infection or continue to die back.

△ **CROSSING BRANCHES**
Cut out any crossing, overcrowded stems. They restrict air circulation and can encourage diseases to develop.

▷ **WHERE TO CUT**
Cut back to a strong, outward-facing bud. Make the cut at an angle, sloping down and away from the bud.

60 PRUNING CLIMBERS

Most climbers benefit from pruning. It prevents them from growing too big and heavy for their supports, and promotes flowers. In general, prune climbers that flower after midsummer in winter or early spring, and those that flower earlier soon after flowering.

▷ **PRUNING HONEYSUCKLE**
Honeysuckles can become extremely tangled and untidy. Trim away dead and damaged stems from beneath the new growth.

△ **REMOVING OLD WOOD**
Old, woody stems rarely flower properly, so are best removed. Prune them to ground level, leaving only healthy new growth.

CONTROLLING CLIMBERS
Prune climbers regularly in order to keep their growth under control. Overgrown climbers may damage walls, guttering, or other structures.

61 CUTTING BACK PERENNIALS

Regular trimming and cutting back are prerequisites for tidy borders. In autumn or early winter, after perennials have flowered, cut the shoots to the base and remove dead or faded stems or leaves. If plants are not fully hardy, leave on the top-growth over winter to protect the crown from frost-heaving, and remove in spring.

KEEPING TIDY
Use hand shears to cut down the dead stems of perennials (such as this Rudbeckia) to ground level, or to just above new growth, in autumn or early winter.

WINTER FEATURE
Some perennials, especially grasses, have attractive foliage or seed-heads. Leave these on over the winter months and remove in spring.

62 TRIMMING HEDGES

Prune hedges with care in the first few years after planting, to encourage even growth. Once established, they need regular trimming to keep their shape. Hand shears are ideal for most trimming jobs, but for larger areas an electric hedgetrimmer is both quicker and easier.

▷ **USING SHEARS**
To ensure that the top of the hedge is flat and level, always hold the blades of the shears parallel to the line of the hedge.

RENOVATING A HEDGE
If a hedge has been neglected or has become overgrown, drastic pruning may be required. Cut back one side only, then cut back the other side the following year.

▷ **USING HEDGETRIMMERS**
Keeping the trimmer blade parallel to the hedge, use a wide, sweeping motion. Remember always to wear protective goggles.

Remove the flowering stem with sharp pruners

63 DEADHEADING

Remove dead flowerheads from annuals, roses, and most perennials: it promotes new growth, and sometimes a second flowering. Deadhead soft-stemmed plants by hand; use pruners for tougher-stemmed plants. Use shears to cut back the top-growth of herbaceous geraniums after flowering.

DEADHEADING A ROSE
After the rose has faded, cut back the stem to a strong shoot or outward-facing bud.

PROTECTING PLANTS

64 COMMON DISEASES: REMEDIES

Familiarize yourself with common plant diseases, and treat them immediately. Many can be prevented by improved growing conditions. If using fungicide, ensure it is the correct type.

▷ **Rust:** *Pick off affected leaves; spray plant with fungicide; prune regularly to improve air circulation; avoid wetting foliage.*

△ **Fungal leafspot:** *Remove affected leaves; spray plant with fungicide; keep in good condition.*

▽ **Botrytis:** *Remove infected tissue; spray plant with fungicide; prune to improve ventilation.*

△ **Powdery mildew:** *Remove affected leaves, stems, or flowers; spray plant with fungicide; prune, mulch, and water plant regularly.*

▷ **Clubroot:** *Discard affected plants; improve drainage and add lime to soil; keep area free of weeds.*

◁ **Viruses (ringspot):** *No cure, so reduce spread: discard infected plants; control disease-carrying pests; observe hygiene.*

65 COMMON PESTS: REMEDIES

Pests can have a devastating effect on plants. Suitable chemical remedies may control the problem. Biological controls (where predators and parasites are introduced to deal with pests) are also effective.

◁ *Slugs & snails: Collect pests; use pellets or drenches, and a nematode parasite for slugs; cultivate soil and clear up debris.*

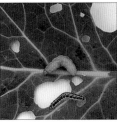

△ *Caterpillars: Pick insects off plant; spray plant with biological control Bacillus thuringiensis or pesticide; cut out damaged stems.*

▷ *Earwigs: Collect pests; place an inverted flowerpot filled with hay on a stake near the plant; spray plant with pesticide.*

△ *Vine weevils: Collect adult beetles and grubs; use a nematode parasite; chemicals are rarely successful.*

▷ *Spider mites: Use the predatory mite Phytoseiulus persimilis or spray plant with pesticide.*

◁ *Aphids: treat plants with insecticidal spray or soap; encourage aphid-eating insects (Tip 66).*

▷ *Flea beetle: Treat the leaves and also soil, if necessary, with pesticide; clear up debris thoroughly.*

66 TEN WAYS TO PREVENT PESTS & DISEASES

1 Buy good-quality plants, and position them in the correct soil and site (*Tip 7*).

2 Use the correct planting distances: congested plants are more prone to diseases, since air circulation is poor.

3 Consider a companion planting plan – certain plant combinations are thought to reduce problems.

4 Water and feed correctly to encourage healthy growth.

5 Prune to create an open-centered crown or branch system to reduce humidity. Remove infected stems.

6 Observe good hygiene: clean containers with hot water and soap; clear away plant debris.

7 Water seeds, seedlings, and young plants with clean water rather than from a barrel.

8 Encourage beneficial garden creatures such as ladybugs, hoverflies, lacewings, spiders, and centipedes: they eat aphids and other pests.

9 Rotate vegetables around a number of plots to avoid buildup of problems in the soil.

10 Inspect plants regularly and treat problems immediately.

67 PROTECTING FROM WIND

Strong or prolonged winds can do extensive damage to plants, causing leaves to brown, wither, and eventually die. Plant trees and hedges for protection, or use a commercial windbreak. Select plants that are tolerant of wind (*Tip 7*). Those with small, thick leaves tend to be more resilient than large- or thin-leaved plants.

TEMPORARY WINDBREAK
Young plants are highly susceptible to damage from strong winds. Protect them with a windbreak of double netting secured with stakes.

WIND TUNNELS
Do not site sheds or greenhouses too close to other structures: wind rushes through gaps, often damaging plants.

68 STAKING

Many plants require staking to keep them firmly in place, particularly in a windy site. Trees are best staked at planting. Drive a single stake about 24in (60cm) below the soil to hold a tree firm. After about two years, the roots will be established and the stake can be removed.

△ STAKING A TREE
Use a vertical stake at planting time. Secure with a buckle-and-spacer tie.

SECURE STAKING
In very windy conditions, or for trees over 12ft (4m) tall, use three stakes in a triangle.

△ ANGLED STAKE
In some cases, stakes may be added after planting – if angled, they will not damage the root ball.

▽ TYING IN
Tall stems or flower spikes often need support. Loosely tie them to stakes, using string or plant ties.

69 PREVENTING HEAT DAMAGE

High temperatures can be fatal. They lead to moisture loss in both plant and soil, which may result in scorching, wilting, and poor nutrient uptake. In areas prone to hot summers, or in heat traps (Tip 4), choose plants that are suited to dry, sunny sites (Tip 7). Add organic matter to the soil to retain moisture.

◁ COVERING UP
Protect young plants from wilting by shielding them from the sun. An inverted flower pot is ideal.

▷ DAMPING DOWN
In very hot weather, wet the greenhouse floor to reduce the temperature and increase humidity.

70 PROTECTING FROM COLD & FROST

One of the greatest threats to many plants, particularly when young, is cold. It causes the most severe damage in early winter, or in early spring when plants have just started into growth. Never site plants that are not fully hardy in frost pockets (*Tip 4*), or feed them too late in the season, since this stimulates growth.

◁ **PROVIDE INSULATION**
Protect a plant and its container from cold: wrap the pot in burlap, bubble plastic, or newspaper, then tie with string.

▷ **PROTECT ROSES**
During winter, mound up soil around rose stems to reach a height of at least 5–6in (12–15cm). Use compost if the soil is heavy.

71 PROTECTING FROM SNOW

Snow can be immensely harmful, particularly when followed by severe cold. Its weight may put a severe strain on hedges, trees, and shrubs, causing them to bend and change their shape, or even snapping off whole branches. To protect woody plants, brush the snow off branches carefully, before it freezes. For small plants, cover them with newspaper or use a cloche. If yours is an area with heavy snowfall, a snow frame may be necessary.

PROTECT YOUR HEDGE
Clipping a hedge so that it tapers slightly toward the top will prevent snow from settling on it and causing damage.

PROTECTION FOR TREES
Tie up the branches of conifers and other densely branched trees with galvanized wire. This stops snow from building up on the branches and also provides protection against wind.

PROPAGATING PLANTS

72 WHY PROPAGATE?

One of the most rewarding aspects of gardening is propagating your own plants. You can collect propagating material from your own garden or from friends, and increase the range of plants in your garden at very little expense. Sowing from seed is the most common method, but there are other simple ways, too: you can divide plants, take cuttings, and propagate by layering.

IMPATIENS

73 USEFUL EQUIPMENT

Most seeds and some cuttings need fairly warm conditions in the early stages. Heated propagators provide a temperature-controlled environment. Cold frames and cloches are useful for hardening off greenhouse-raised plants before planting outdoors.

△ IMPROVISED MINI-CLOCHE
If you don't have a propagator, use a clear plastic bag instead. Harden off the cuttings gradually by cutting the corners of the bag.

▽ HEATED PROPAGATOR
With a heated propagator, you can raise a wide range of plants starting early in the year.

51

74 SOWING SEEDS IN A TRAY

Planting seeds in trays gives you maximum control over their growing conditions before planting out. This is especially useful for marginally hardy plants, or those with specific needs. They may be kept in a greenhouse, propagator, or cold frame, or indoors. The sowing time depends on the seed type. Check the packet for details.

1 Sieve seed soil mix into a tray, and water. Sprinkle the seeds evenly by tapping them from a folded piece of paper.

2 Place a fine layer of sieved soil mix over the seeds, then a fine layer of grit. Label and store at a suitable temperature.

3 Once the seedlings are large enough to handle, lift them out. Hold them carefully by the seed leaves.

75 SOWING SEEDS IN A FLOWERBED

There are numerous seeds that can be sown directly into a flowerbed or border. Many annuals, including a number of wildflowers, are especially easy to grow in this way. After sowing, clearly label where and what the seeds are.

SUITABLE PLANTS

Amaranthus caudatus	Cosmos bipinnatus
Brachyscome iberidifolia	Gypsophila elegans
Calendula officinalis	Iberis umbellata
Centaurea cyanus	Linaria maroccana
Clarkia elegans	Nemophila menziesii
Cleome hassleriana	Nigella damascena
Convolvulus tricolor	Papaver rhoeas

1 Rake, weed, and water the soil. Sprinkle an outline with sand to mark where to sow, then sow the seeds in rows marked by the sand.

PROTECTING SEEDS
Wire netting over seeds keeps animals at bay. A sheet of glass protects sensitive seeds against excessive moisture loss.

Hold by seed leaves

4 Transfer the seedlings into pots or trays. Grow on and harden off the seedlings before planting out.

76 SOWING VEGETABLE BEDS

You may not have enough space in your garden to devote an entire bed to vegetables, but you can always grow them between other plants in an ornamental border. Prepare the soil by adding organic matter and fertilizer before sowing, and water and feed often. To prevent damping-off disease, water with a copper-based fungicide and rotate crops regularly. Check the packets for individual seed requirements.

1 △ Use two stakes with string between to make a straight line. Draw a stake along the string to mark out a row.

2 △ Sprinkle some seeds along the row, and cover with soil. Use the back of the rake to tamp down the soil gently.

▷ **KITCHEN GARDEN**
Closer spacing of seeds gives maximum produce in a small space, but keep the site free of weeds.

2 Gently rake soil over the seeds. Keep the ground moist and weed-free. Later, thin the seedlings to the spacing indicated on the packet.

GROWING IN CONTAINERS
Peppers, tomatoes, and cucumbers can be raised in pots or grown in bags on patios. Lettuces can be grown in windowboxes.

77 DIVIDING PERENNIALS

One of the simplest and least expensive ways of increasing plants in your garden is to divide them. It enables you to produce several healthy new plants from one established clump, and also rejuvenates the clump itself if you cut away dead or weak growth and remove weeds growing through the roots. Late autumn or early spring is generally the best time to divide most perennials, but avoid extreme weather conditions. If your soil is very heavy, divide in spring.

SUITABLE PLANTS

Achillea
Aconitum
Adenophora
Aster (some)
Astilbe
Astrantia
Campanula (some)
Coreopsis
Crambe cordifolia
Dicentra
Doronicum
Helianthus
Helleborus orientalis
Hemerocallis
Heuchera
Hosta
Liatris
Lychnis
Lythrum
Nepeta
Ophiopogon
Phlox
Physostegia
Polemonium
Primula (some)
Pulmonaria
Saponaria
Scabiosa caucasica
Sedum spectabile & cultivars
Thalictrum
Trollius
Veronica

1 △ Ease the roots out with a fork and lift the plant. This plant is dying in the center, but the outer parts will provide several new plants.

2 △ Gently tease the clump apart by hand: you will be able to see or feel where to divide it. Each section should have a healthy root system.

▽ USING HAND FORKS
For small, fibrous-rooted perennials, it may be easier to divide plants using two hand forks back to back.

▷ USING A SPADE
Divide tough, fleshy-rooted plants with a spade in spring. Each division must include several buds.

78 DIVIDING RHIZOMES

Several rhizomatous plants, with thick, fleshy rhizomes, are very easy to divide. Do this in autumn or spring, using a fork to ease out the clump. Some rhizomes, such as bergenias, should be replanted so that they are buried in the soil, with the top-growth above ground. Others, such as irises, should be barely exposed.

SUITABLE PLANTS
Anemone hupehensis
Bergenia
Iris
Schizostylis

1 ◁ Shake off the soil. Pull the rhizomes apart into easy to handle sections. If the clump is congested, use a knife.

2 ▷ Discard old or diseased rhizomes and select healthy ones, each with at least one bud. Trim off damaged ends.

3 ▽ Trim long roots by one-third. Cut back the foliage of irises to about 6in (15cm). Plant the sections 12in (30cm) apart.

3 △ Replant divided sections immediately. Trim off any old, large, or damaged leaves to reduce moisture loss. Replant, refirm, and water in well.

SUITABLE BULBS
Allium (some)
Alstroemeria
Arum (some)
Crinum (some)
Crocus
Fritillaria (some)
Galanthus
Gladiolus (some)
Hyacinthus
Iris Juno group,
  I. Reticulata group (some)
Lilium
Muscari
Narcissus
Nerine (some)
Tulipa

79 DIVIDING BULBS

Bulbs produce offsets around the base of the parent bulb. If they are overcrowded, they will not flower well. Separate the offsets and replant them for a healthy new supply. Divide most bulbs when the foliage is dying back.

1 Remove the bulbs from the clump of soil. Discard any that are dead or diseased.

2 Separate large offsets or pairs of bulbs. Take off the loose outer layers. Replant immediately.

80 TAKING SOFTWOOD CUTTINGS

Perennials and most shrubs may be propagated by taking softwood cuttings. In spring, take a 3–5in (7–12cm) cutting from the soft growth at the top of the stem with a sharp knife, making a cut just below a leaf node. Remove the lowest pair of leaves.

SUITABLE PLANTS
Abelia
Abutilon
Clematis
Forsythia
Fuchsia
Hydrangea
Impatiens (some)
Lonicera
Lupinus
Parthenocissus
Pelargonium
Viburnum

1 Bend wire netting over a jar of water. Insert cuttings and place the jar in a light spot.

2 When roots have developed, remove the plants and pot up in small pots of soil mix.

81 TAKING SEMI-RIPE CUTTINGS

Take semi-ripe cuttings in mid- to late summer for trees, shrubs, and roses. Choose healthy sideshoots that are soft at the top and just hard at the base, from stems of the current year's growth.

As with all cuttings, prevent moisture loss by keeping them in a plastic bag before use, and cut the leaves of larger-leaved plants in half across their width before inserting the cuttings in soil mix.

1 ◁ Trim a stem into several cuttings, each about 3–6in (7–15cm) long, and sever each below a node. On one side of the base of the cutting, slice away a strip of bark 1–1½in (2.5–4cm) long.

2 ◁ Dip the base of each cutting in hormone rooting powder. Insert each one into a pot of cutting soil mix or multi-purpose mix and keep in a propagator, cold frame, or greenhouse.

3 △ Once they are well rooted, carefully lift the cuttings and transfer them into individual pots. Gradually harden them off before growing them on in their pots or planting out.

SUITABLE PLANTS

Abutilon	Clematis	Lavandula
Andromeda	Cupressus	Mahonia
Aucuba	Cytisus	Philadelphus
Berberis	Daphne	Pieris
Camellia	Deutzia	Rhododendron
Ceanothus	Elaeagnus	Skimmia
Choisya	Ilex	Viburnum
Cistus	Juniperus	Weigela

82 TAKING ROOT CUTTINGS

When dormant in autumn or early spring, lift young plants and tease out the roots. With larger plants, expose only part of the root system. Take roots of ¼in (5mm) or more in diameter, close to the main stem, and remove laterals. Cuttings should be 2–6in (5–15cm) long, so take several from one root.

1 ◁ Make a straight cut where the root was severed from the plant, and an angled cut at the other end. Repeat along the root's length.

Space cuttings 2in (5cm) apart

2 △ Place the cuttings, angled cut down, in soil mix, with the tips just showing. Cover with ⅛in (3mm) of grit.

SUITABLE PLANTS

Acanthus	Erodium
Aesculus parviflora	Gypsophila
Anemone x hybrida	Papaver orientale
Aralia	Phlox
Campanula	Rhus
Clerodendron	Trollius
Echinops	Verbascum

83 LAYERING

You can propagate numerous common trees, shrubs, and climbers by layering. There are many different ways to do this: one simple technique is shown here. Layer between autumn and spring, and choose a flexible stem that you can bend down to the ground.

1 ◁ Make an angled cut on the lower side of the stem. Cut about halfway into the stem to form a "tongue."

2 ▷ Dip the cut stem end in hormone rooting powder. Ensure that the powder gets right inside the cut area.

3 ◁ Place the cut area into a pot of soil mix. Keep it in place with a metal peg or bent wire. Pot up when rooted.

SUITABLE PLANTS

Andromeda	Magnolia
Aucuba	Passiflora (most)
Chaenomeles	Rhododendron
Erica	Rosa
Fothergilla	Syringa
Lonicera	Wisteria

84 TAKING HARDWOOD CUTTINGS

Many deciduous and evergreen shrubs, as well as some soft fruits, can be easily raised from hardwood cuttings. Take cuttings between mid-autumn and early winter, and use strong, fully ripe or hardened stem growths produced during the current season. If taking cuttings from deciduous shrubs, wait until just after the leaves have fallen. Keep hardwood cuttings in a prepared bed or trench outside, or in containers in a cold frame. They should root sufficiently in approximately six to twelve months.

SUITABLE PLANTS
Buddleja
Buxus
Euonymus
Forsythia
Kerria
Philadelphus
Ribes
Salix
Spiraea
Weigela

2 △ Cut the stem into 6in (15cm) lengths. Dip the base of each length into hormone rooting powder.

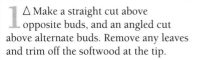

Straight cut just above opposite buds

1 △ Make a straight cut above opposite buds, and an angled cut above alternate buds. Remove any leaves and trim off the softwood at the tip.

3 △ Place the cuttings into pots of cutting soil mix so that about 1–2in (2.5–5cm) is showing. Label the pots, and place them in a cold frame.

GROWING IN CONTAINERS

85 CONTAINERS OUTSIDE

Containers add a splash of color to patios and balconies. Their main advantage is that they are easy to move around: use them as a focal point when the plants are at their best, and move them to a less prominent place when past their prime. Containers also enable you to grow plants that may not tolerate certain conditions in your garden, such as an alkaline soil.

DISPLAY IN SEMI-SHADE

86 WHICH CONTAINER?

Containers must be large enough to allow root development, but not so large that they look bottom-heavy, or are too heavy to move when filled with soil and plants. Small pots dry out more quickly.

▷ *Hanging baskets are best made of plastic-coated wire. They are available in a range of sizes.*

▽ *Wooden half-barrels provide good insulation in winter but can be heavy and need regular maintenance.*

▽ *Plastic containers are inexpensive, lightweight, and easy to maintain. They are also weather resistant.*

△ *Terracotta pots suit most sites, and weather attractively. They tend to be fairly heavy and stable.*

87 DRAINAGE

Good drainage is essential for healthy container-grown plants. If drainage is poor, the plant's roots will become soggy and rot. Check that your pot has enough holes to let excess moisture drain away, and add more if necessary. Keep drainage holes clear of garden debris.

FEET & SAUCERS
Use terracotta or china feet beneath a pot to keep holes free of debris. Saucers may also be used, but they hold water and may cause waterlogging.

DRILL HOLES
If the drainage holes in your container have not been punched out properly, use a drill to do it yourself.

ADD A DRAINAGE LAYER
To create a drainage layer, place broken pots or used teabags in the bottom of the pot before planting.

KEEP HOLES CLEAR
Place bricks under the base of a half-barrel to raise it off the ground and keep drainage holes clear.

88 PLANTING SUBSTANCES

Peat and peat-substitute soil mixes are good for short-term use, but dry out quickly. Soil-based mixtures are heavier, but may easily get compacted. Slow-release fertilizers give out nutrients gradually. Water-retaining granules absorb, then release, water when soil mix dries out.

△ SLOW-RELEASE FERTILIZER GRANULES

△ SOIL-BASED MIX

△ PEAT-BASED SOIL MIX

△ COIR SOIL MIX

△ WATER-RETAINING GRANULES

89 BASIC PLANTING METHOD

Whatever the container (here a window-box), the planting method is the same. Before you begin, scrub the container with disinfectant; rinse well. Water plants, soil mix, and porous containers.

1 △ Half-fill the windowbox with soil mix plus slow-release fertilizer and water-retaining granules. Remove the plants from their pots.

2 △ Carefully loosen the root balls of the plants. Place them in the box, allowing ½in (1cm) between the necks of the plants and the top of the box.

3 △ Add soil mix between the plants and firm the root balls. Water, allow to settle, then fill any gaps with soil mix.

▽ LAVISH DISPLAY
Containers are most impressive filled with an abundance of closely spaced plants. Feed, water, and deadhead regularly.

Trailing plants placed around edges

90 PLANTING A HANGING BASKET

To provide instant color in areas that are frequently neglected – house and garage walls, porches, or balconies – hanging baskets can't be bettered. The key to their success is a sheltered site, good planting, and frequent watering and feeding. They are available in various sizes. Avoid very small sizes, which dry out very quickly.

1 △ Line the basket with sphagnum moss until it covers the base of the basket completely.

2 △ Place a plastic liner over the moss. Unless planting in the base, cut some drainage holes in it.

3 △ If using trailing plants at the base, wrap each plant in plastic shaped into a cone.

4 △ Pierce a hole in the base. From the inside, push the plant in plastic through the holes. Peel away the plastic.

5 ▽ Build up layers of trailing plants, adding soil mix between each layer. Plant the top with trailing and bushy plants. Hang in position and water well.

BASKET LINERS
Foam, felt, and coir make alternative, more environmentally friendly basket liners than moss.

LAWNS

91 SOWING A LAWN

Sowing is less expensive than sodding, but you will need to wait for at least ten weeks before using your new lawn. Select a seed that suits your site and needs. Before you begin, clear away debris and weeds, dig over, add fertilizer, and firm the area by treading evenly. Mark some pegs, each at the same distance from the top.
- Sow in warm, moist conditions, in autumn or early spring.

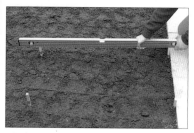

1 △ Firm the soil. Drive in parallel rows of pegs, with the markings at the required level of the lawn. Check the pegs are level and adjust if necessary.

2 △ Rake the soil to the level of the markings on the pegs. When the soil is level, remove the pegs, firm the soil again, then rake in a granular fertilizer.

3 △ Using pots, mark out an area of 3ft (1m) square. Weigh out the seed needed for this area and scatter it evenly from a pot. Repeat for the whole lawn.

4 △ Once you have sown the whole lawn, lightly rake a thin layer of soil over the seed. Water the lawn frequently with a fine sprinkler.

92 SODDING A LAWN

A newly sodded lawn creates instant impact and can usually be used within two months. Select good-quality sod suited to the site and level of wear the lawn will receive. As with sowing, thorough preparation of the site is essential. Lay sod within two days of buying.
■ Lay sod in any season, when the soil is moist. Avoid very dry, wet, hot, or cold conditions.

SPRIGS & PLUGS
In some areas, grass stolons or rhizomes, known as sprigs, or small plugs of sod, are used instead of sod pieces. Scatter sprigs or plant plugs in spring or in early autumn.

1 Sod will be delivered rolled or stacked flat. If you are not able to lay the sod right away, keep it in a shady spot.

2 Lay the first row of sod along a straight edge. Roll out each piece, staggering the joints to give an even finish. Repeat.

3 Firm down the sod with the back of a rake. Brush a sandy top-dressing into any gaps. Water frequently.

93 WHEN & HOW TO FEED

For lush green grass, regular feeding is essential. Consider using a lawn fertilizer that includes weedkiller. Follow the instructions on the bag for rates. Water well.
■ Feed the lawn in spring with a high-nitrogen fertilizer, and again in early autumn – after scarifying and aerating (*Tips 98 & 99*) – with a fertilizer containing nitrogen, phosphorus, potassium, and iron.

APPLYING GRANULAR FERTILIZER
Scatter the granules within an area 3ft (1m) square, marked out with pots.

94 CONTROLLING WEEDS

Lawn weeds are inevitable, even in a very well-maintained lawn. A small number of large weeds can be removed by hand as they appear, preferably before they spread. For lawns with a variety of small weeds, a chemical weedkiller is usually the best solution. Lawn weedkillers are selective and do not harm lawn grasses. The rates and method of use depend on the product, so always read the instructions on the package carefully.

■ Use weedkiller in spring or summer, shortly after or while fertilizing.

SELFHEAL

WEEDING DANDELIONS
Lever dandelions out of the lawn using a knife. Remove the whole root. Firm back the soil.

NEW LAWNS
Do not use weedkiller on new lawns for a minimum of six months.

95 COMMON LAWN PROBLEMS

■ Moss: Rake out moss and consider improving drainage. Aerate regularly (*Tip 98*) and top-dress (*Tip 100*).
■ Moles: Burrowing moles cause molehills. Use mole smokes or trap them.
■ Grubs: The larvae of several beetles may infest grass. The grubs eat the roots, causing the grass to turn yellow and die. Treat with an insecticide or use milky-spore disease (a biological control); it may take a year to become effective.
■ Drought: The lawn is discolored in areas or all over. Water often, feed in the evening, let the grass grow longer than usual, and lightly feed after recovery.
■ Snow mold: Yellowish patches develop and, in moist weather, a white or pink fungal growth appears. Aerate and scarify regularly (*Tips 98 & 99*), and treat with fungicide.

DOGS
Brown scorch marks on a lawn may be caused by dog urine. Foxes may also enter gardens and foul lawns.

96 MOWING

Cut grass to about ½–1in (1–2.5cm). A rotary mower is fine for most lawns, but for a high-quality cut, use a reel mower.

- Mow as soon as needed (often once a week in summer). Avoid mowing when the ground is very wet, or in very hot or dry weather or during frosty conditions.

ATTRACTIVE PROSPECT
For a healthy lawn, regular mowing is essential. It encourages dense growth, which helps to restrict weeds and moss.

97 MAINTAINING EDGES

Ragged edges can spoil the effect of a well-maintained lawn. To neaten them, use long-handled shears. You could also use a nylon-line trimmer: it will do the job faster but may leave slightly ragged edges. Once lawn edges collapse, or are very irregular, you will need to recut them with a half-moon edger. Make sure tools are very sharp, and hold them upright to make a clean line.

- Trim the edges regularly. Recut once or twice a year.

TRIM THE EDGES
To remove grass overhanging the edge of the lawn, use long-handled edging shears held upright. Alternatively, use a nylon-line trimmer with an adjustable head.

RECUT THE EDGES
Neaten up irregular edges using a half-moon edger. Lay a board to give you a straight edge. Holding the edger vertically, cut against the side of the board.

98 AERATING

When a lawn becomes compacted, in particular during very wet weather, the turf can die off and mosses may grow. Aerating a lawn improves drainage by making it less compacted, and stimulates healthy growth.

Most lawns need aerating only every two or three years, but in areas of heavy traffic you may need to do it annually. Use a garden fork or, for large areas, a hollow-tined aerator.

- Aerate in autumn, after mowing, then apply a top-dressing (*Tip 100*).

AERATING THE LAWN
Drive a fork into the lawn to 4in (10cm) deep. Gently ease it back and forth.

99 SCARIFYING

If left unchecked, organic debris builds up on a lawn, restricting air circulation and preventing water and fertilizers from reaching the grass roots. Scarifying is the removal of this debris: it thins the lawn and enables healthy new grass to grow. Kill off any moss before you begin, or it will spread to new areas.

- Scarify in autumn, when the soil is just moist.

▷ **SCARIFYING GRASS**
Rake vigorously with a spring-tined rake. The tines should reach the soil surface.

△ **AFTER SCARIFYING**
Although a lawn always looks worse after scarifying than before, its beautiful appearance in spring will reward all your effort.

100 TOP-DRESSING

An unhealthy lawn is often the result of poor drainage. After aerating, work top-dressing into the holes to improve drainage. You can buy a top-dressing mixture or make it up yourself, using the ingredients below.

- Top-dress in autumn, ideally on a dry day.

△ 6 PARTS SHARP HORTICULTURAL SAND

▷ 3 PARTS SIEVED, GOOD-QUALITY SOIL

△ 1 PART WELL-ROTTED ORGANIC MATTER

△ **APPLYING TOP-DRESSING**
Use a spade or shovel to spread the top-dressing over the lawn, then brush it in with a garden broom.

101 LAWN RENOVATION

Lawns receive a great deal of wear, particularly if exposed to heavy use. Carry out a program of regular maintenance, and deal with problems as soon as they occur. If resowing or resodding, use the same mixture of seed or type of sod as the original.

- Renovate in spring, late summer, or early autumn.

REPAIRING EDGES
Damaged edges can ruin the appearance of a lawn. However, small areas of edging are easy to repair.

WEAR & TEAR
To help protect grass in play areas, such as under a swing, secure sturdy netting to the ground with U-shaped staples.

1 Cut out a rectangular piece of sod around the damaged edge. Turn it until the damaged area faces inward. Firm well.

2 Add a sandy soil mixture to the soil in the damaged area until level with the lawn soil, then reseed. Water well.

INDEX

Acknowledgments

Dorling Kindersley would like to thank Hilary Bird for
compiling the index, Alison Copland for proofreading,
Richard Hammond for editorial assistance, and
Robert Campbell and Mark Bracey for DTP assistance.

Photography
KEY: t *top*; b *bottom*; c *center*; l *left*; r *right*
All photographs by Peter Anderson, Jerry Harpur,
Stephen Hayward, Jane Stockman, Matthew Ward, Steven Wooster,
and Jerry Young except: Eric Crichton Photos 37t.

Illustrations
Kuo Kang Chen, Karen Cochrane, and John Woodcock.